In Bending Our Ear Downward

Seven Poems on Czech Jewish Cemeteries (židovský hřbitov)

Neil O. Anderson

Minnesota Libraries Publishing Project, https://mlpp.pressbooks.pub/
2019

Cover Photograph. Interpretive gate to the židovský hřbitov (Jewish Cemetery) in Třeboň, Czech Republic, with a sympathy floral design created by Neil O. Anderson in honor of the completion of our 2010-2011 Fulbright research in the Czech Republic (left to right: Neil O. Anderson, Lynn Silverman, and Mark Gilquist), May 2011. Photo Credit: Neil O. Anderson; graphic design: Andrew J. Stobbs.

First Printing: 2019

Library of Congress Control Number: 2019921244

ISBN: 978-0-578-62130-2

Minnesota Libraries Publishing Project,

Pressbooks Public Self-Publishing Platform

https://mlpp.pressbooks.pub/

Ordering Information:

A hardcopy of the book may be ordered from:

 https://mlpp.pressbooks.pub/inbendingoureardownward/

Special discounts are available on quantity purchases by corporations, associations, educators, and others. For details, contact the publisher at the above listed link.

U.S. trade bookstores and wholesalers: Please contact the Minnesota Libraries Publishing Project, weblink: https://mlpp.pressbooks.pub/

Dedication

In Bending Our Ear Downward is lovingly dedicated to my late husband, Mark E. Gilquist. Thank you for your undying love, inspiration, support, and dedication to our adventures in the Czech Republic that made all of this possible. I love you!

Figure 1. Mark photographing at Markvarec cemetery. Photo Credit: Neil Anderson.

Contents

Acknowledgements

I would like to thank the United States, Department of State, Bureau of Educational and Cultural Affairs, J. William Fulbright Scholar Program[1] and the Czech Fulbright Program[2], for funding my 2010-2011 research/teaching scholarship in the Czech Republic which opened the doors to creating this book. Teaching courses at the University of South Bohemia (České Budějovice, Czech Republic) and adventuring on plant collection trips for genetic research on the native wetland plant, *Phalaris arundinacea* (reed canarygrass), afforded Mark Gilquist and I numerous opportunities to also see vestiges of Jewish life throughout Czech culture.

Through a series of contacts in the Czech Fulbright Program, we joined in Lynn Silverman's[3] Fulbright research to adventure together to specific Jewish cemeteries for photographic portraits. In joining in the spirit of these adventures, our own series of photographs and, ultimately, my poetry, arose to create this artistic endeavor. Thank you Lynn for your work, your inspiration, and creation of this journey!

This work would also not have been possible without the knowledge, wisdom and devotee to the history of the Czech Republic, Dr. Jan (Hony) Květ[4], a colleague that spawned my Fulbright. Hony directed us to find several of the Jewish cemeteries as well as providing contacts and relevant historical data concerning the sites. Thank you, Hony!

The Czech Fulbright Executive Director (Dr. Hanka Ripková) and office staff (Hana Rambousková, Miloš Frieb, Andrea Semancová, Jakub Tešar, Zuzana Votočková) embedded us in the

[1] Office of Academic Exchange Programs, Bureau of Educational and Cultural Affairs, United States Department of State; Website: http://fulbright.state.gov
[2] Commission JW Fulbright, Karmelitská 17 118 00, Prague 1, Czech Republic, E-mail: fulbright@fulbright.cz, http://fulbright.cz
[3] Professor of Photography, Maryland Institute College of Art, Baltimore, MD USA; https://lynnsilverman.com/
[4] Professor Emeritus, University of South Bohemia, Faculty of Science, Branišovská 31, 370 05 České Budějovice, Czech Republic; Czech Academy of Sciences, Czech Globe, Centre for Global Change Research, 370 05 České Budějovice, Czech Republic

Czech culture and aspects of daily life that made our venturing into remote regions possible throughout our Fulbright stay. Thank you for your dedication to international academic and scholarly exchange! Long may it continue.

After our return to the United States, we worked on submitting a proposal to the Weisman Art Museum (WAM) for an exhibition to highlight our Fulbright experiences. Sadly, prior to realizing the exhibition at WAM, Mark passed away in 2014. Thank you, Mark, for your devotion to this project! You are forever in our hearts.

Our resulting exhibition, "Still...life", in WAM's Target Gallery during December 2015 – August 2016 and my poetry reading during the show all owe a debt of gratitude to the WAM staff! Special thanks for infinite amounts of help in the process are extended to: Dr. Lyndel King, Director and Chief Curator; Diane Mullin, Senior Curator; Christopher Williams, Senior Preparator & Exhibition Designer; Gwen Sutter, Associate Director for Administration.

Introduction

In ~995 A.D., Jews came to what is now known as the Czech Republic (encompassing modern-day provinces of Bohemia, Moravia, and the region of Silesia)[5]. While they were accepted initially, the period of the Crusades were anti-Semitic with acts of forced baptism into Christianity or … murder. Jews were also forbidden from owning land or conducting business.

When Catholicism expanded its influence during the 13th century, conditions changed for the Jews and their influence increased. This period was short-lived, however, as a resurgence of anti-Semitism included burning Jews at the stake (1389) and the complete expulsion of Jews (1541) when the Habsburg dynasty came to power under Austrian Archduke Ferdinand. Thus, the more recent periods of Nazi anti-Semitism and Soviet neglect were not unfamiliar to European Jewry, even though the severity surpassed all previous attempts to exterminate them.

It is a poignant irony that the Czech Republic is one of the richest countries of Jewish sites and artifacts. Ironic, because Czechoslovakia (as it was then called), according to the plans laid out by Hitler, was to house a museum of Judaica confiscated during the transportation of the Jews to extermination camps. This monument to what was to be a vanished race has become known as the "Precious Legacy". Spared from being bombed during WWII, Prague and the surrounding countryside of Bohemia and Moravia contain over three hundred buildings and cemetery sites (židovský hřbitov) and represent the largest vestige of Jewish culture and heritage found in Central and Eastern Europe.

This collection of poems is the result of a joint project between myself (a Horticultural Science Professor, University of Minnesota) and Lynn Silverman (Professor in Photography, Maryland Institute College of Art) while we were in the Czech Republic as J. William

---

[5] Czech Republic Virtual Jewish History Tour. Jewish Virtual Library. https://www.jewishvirtuallibrary.org/czech-republic-virtual-jewish-history-tour

Fulbright Scholars in 2010-2011. Together with my late husband, Mark E. Gilquist (Mathematics Professor, Anoka-Hennepin School District, ISD-11, Minnesota), we explored a number of cemeteries during that year, each with our own particular agenda. We three artists traveled to Jewish cemeteries (židovský hřbitov in Czech) around Bohemia and Moravia as an alternate way to explore the history of the Holocaust instead of visiting the better-known concentration camps in the Czech Republic and Poland. Although many of the graveyards are locked to deter vandalism, a number were accessible. I discovered and recorded plants used for sympathy thriving in these abandoned oases. From his unique wheelchair vantage point, Mark photographed details of the stonewall construction and grave markers as well as some of the plants. Lynn's response to the lack of access was to explore the periphery of these sites. Each cemetery's boundary wall, rather than the headstones, becomes the defining feature that draws attention to the particular history of the place and its incorporation into the surrounding area.

Today's židovský hřbitov represent remnants of monuments to past Jewish citizenry, in various stages of restoration from Nazi destruction and Soviet neglect. All židovský hřbitov were located outside of the walls of the ancient towns and cities, separate from the Christian cemeteries. In only one instance, at Ceske Krumlov, are these two cemeteries adjacent; here the Christian cemetery completely surrounds the židovský hřbitov.

The process of finding each židovský hřbitov involved a series of preplanning research efforts, locating them on modern Czech maps, engaging local historians, and often asking local residents if they knew of their location. At least one of the cemeteries we could never locate. As we discovered each cemetery, many of which were buried deep in forests with minimal road access, we realized that they had characteristic looks. Typically, the architectural designs for each cemetery were the walls – either made from native stone (the ancient ones), brick or brick-faced with stucco (more recent). The walls were typically topped with a flat or angled layer of red brick or terra cotta roofing tiles with corners and gateposts rising higher than the walls and capped with the same materials. A Ceremonial House was located within the walls of smaller sites or incorporated into the wall at larger ones.

It is ironic that, despite the decades-long period of Nazi destruction and Soviet neglect, plants survive in abundance and have overtaken many of these sites. They could not be annihilated. Thus, plants appear and recur in all of these poems. Current day plants found at the Jewish cemeteries are not necessarily those directly planted in perennial or eternal sympathy remembrances, although many had linden trees (*Tilia;* Czech: lípa) – the Czech national tree – that were clearly planted in a landscape design. For example, many mature trees are located within the cemetery walls growing upon grave sites. Due to the similarity of these trees with the local forests, these are highly likely to have arisen from seeds of the trees in adjacent or surrounding forests. In other cases, native herbaceous perennials, such as Lily-of-the-valley (*Convallaria majalis*) and English ivy (*Hedera helix*), were already growing in the location where the cemetery was built.

What emerged from our perspectives is how the impact of the present (whether it be the profusion of ivy spilling over the boundary walls, a blind man making his way along an adjacent sidewalk, the seasonal flowering of plants, a random burst of sunshine, amongst other details) colors our perception of these židovský hřbitov. As we continued to gather photographs, it became apparent that our joint venture was developing into a more nuanced view of these sites. This resulted in our photographic and living plant exhibition, ***Still...Life***, in the Target Gallery at the Weisman Art Museum, University of Minnesota, Minneapolis, MN, during December 2015 – August 2016[6].

After visits to seven of the židovský hřbitov sites (we visited far more), in reflecting on each unique experience of visiting and photographing each cemetery, I wrote poems to encapsulate my sense of my place in each of these historic sites. Each resonated with their own history, destructive past, partial restoration and exuded modern-

[6] Skinner, Quinton. Living Testimony: "Still . . . Life" at the Weisman Art Museum Examines the Stillness of Cemeteries. Minnesota Monthly. 50(1) p.26. January 2016. https://www.minnesotamonthly.com/arts-entertainment/still-life-at-the-weisman-art-museum-examines-the-stillness-of-cemeteries/

day desecration. This had to be recorded! Thus, on 18 May 2016, during the **Still...Life** exhibition, I read each of the poems from seven Czech Jewish cemeteries in a Poetry Reading. After each poem I presented some of the history and photographs for each cemetery to provide additional context. This, in its entirety, is what is contained in this monograph, **In Bending Our Ear Downward**.

Neil O. Anderson

In Bending Our Ear Downward

[Rožmberk nad Vltavou, 27 Feb. 2011][7]

In coming here,
cold of stone on stone
lifts in rays,
to where spring weeps
of maples.
Now and then.

Alder buds,
coppered catkin pairs,
pendulously twist
'twixt headstones,
sky.
In this breath of a cemetery:
triangulating
between farm – river – highway
edging Bohemia, Austria.

Now,
in February stillness,
the blanket of wet snows
drowns voices,
summer boaters on Vltavou River –
joyous annual campers,
buoyant rapids enrafted.
Drifting in,
then out.

---

[7] Note: This poem was originally published on our blog:
http://czechfoodiesmn.blogspot.com/2011/03/visit-to-jewish-cemetery-zidovsky_1428.html

The slow melting of snows
on hillside's sunny warmth
drip consciousness
as we read glistening, green lichens
Hebrewed in headstones,
marking
Jews of late.

In bending our ear downward
we hear voices
muffled beneath,
past summer's rush of cars,
rafts,
tractors:
We,
too,
Bohemian winters endured,
bones ache now of dampness cold,
toes still dancing winter's rhythms away.
Near-forgotten sorrows
melt us
in our tracks.

Lest death
should likewise silence
voices lying here,
we lift your eyes,
focus your arms
in embrace
of richness of rivers,
Bohemian forests.
'til summer bursts on Vltavou.

Figure 2. Catkins twirl above the cemetery wall. Photo Credit: Neil Anderson.

Background on the Rožmberk nad Vltavou židovský hřbitov

The Rosenberg family was one of most influential noble families in ancient Bohemia, holding positions in the imperial court and having a lasting influence on the region. Thus, this town in southern Bohemia is named as "Rosenbergs on the Voltava River". The family emblem is a red five-petaled rose against a green field background. We saw this rose occur on old headstones or židovský hřbitov gates (in Třeboň, for example, *cf.* this book's cover photograph) for obvious reasons.

While we don't know exactly when the Jews arrived in Rožmberk nad Vltavou, they were present during the 300-year reign of the Rosenberg family, which commenced in the 1200s. History records a disagreement occurring in 1378 concerning direct transport of kosher meat from Rožmberk into Linz, Austria (just a short distance away) while skipping the tolls in Freistadt, Germany. A subsequent immigration of Jews occurred in 1670 after they were forced out of Vienna. Nonetheless, Rožmberk was a provincial town with a significant Jewish population situated below the castle on the shores of the Voltava River. This is where the original, old židovský hřbitov[8] can be found (founded prior to 1480) although its presence is unmarked and difficult to find due to the fact that it is now a yard with the prayer house now someone's home. The oldest tombstone in this cemetery (1793) is for David Linz who met his fate in the Linz, Austria marketplace[9]. Until 1863 every Jew from Linz was buried here.

Near the end of 19th century, a newer Jewish cemetery was built north of Rožmberk near the road to Český Krumlov where ~100 people are buried. It was here that Dolfi Sternschein was buried in 1935[10], as the final Hebrew laid to rest and >1,000 people, both Christians and Jews, came to his burial to give him final accolades. All other members of his family were subsequently annihilated in the Nazi extermination camps. This is the cemetery that we visited in 2010-2011 since we had tried, but failed, to find the old cemetery. Lynn Silvermann and I finally found the old cemetery during a revisit in 2015.

---

[8] Mrázek, Lubor. The tombstone at the Jewish cemetary in Rožmberk nad Vltavou, dating from 1598. http://www.ckrumlov.info/img.php?img=8027&LANG=en

[9] History Linz https://stadtgeschichte.linz.at/english/

[10] History of Jews in Rožmberk nad Vltavou. Český Krumlov Tourism. Encyclopedia. http://www.encyklopedie.ckrumlov.cz/docs/en/region_histor_hiszid.xml

[Type here]

Continuing Business As Usual

[České Budějovice, 24 Feb. 2011][11]

Hardly
a quiet place of rest.
For anyone.
At the very corner
of metal fencing above,
rusting stone walls surround.

Wrought-iron gates
dispelling
long trailers,
clambering brewery trucks
belching diesel smoke
backwards
into parking spaces:
Over the wall.

A never-ending fluidity
flows the westward wall,
aligning oaks
parked
both within,
without.

---

[11] Note: Originally published on our blog:
http://czechfoodiesmn.blogspot.com/2011/03/visit-to-jewish-cemetery-zidovsky_06.html

Browned,
old *Humulus lupulus*
(hops),
gently quakes,
sprawling in frozen time,
across windswept,
stark,
cold walls:
Noisy soliloquy
of Budvar-laden trucks
parked
out the gates.

Eastward
old gardener's cottages
weather
lost vegetable plots
feeding,
now,
this industrial ecosystem:
Harbinger
of corrugated,
metal-enfolded
truck repair shops.
It is like none other.

Lest we cast
on sleepless rest,
dispersions
on those herein,
perhaps
surround of commerce
is respite
from
continuing
business as usual.

Figure 3. The Ceremonial House brightens in the winter sun against the starkness of the sky. Photo Credit: Mark Gilquist.

Figure 4. An old hops vine (*Humulus lupulus*) dried during the winter and now clings to the walls in desperation. Photo Credit: Neil Anderson.

Background on the České Budějovice židovský hřbitov

The oldest medieval Jewish cemetery in České Budějovice was at a different location than the current one which we visited. The original cemetery perished forever after the expulsion of the Jewish community in 1505-1506[12] . In 1848, Baron Sattelberg purchased land for the current židovský hřbitov, on Bakery Street (6,489 m²). The first burial occurred here in 1867 and ~1300 Jewish citizens were buried here until 1942[13].

This Jewish cemetery was devastated during the Nazi occupation and some of the finer tombstones and stonework were taken (later ground up and used as stone paths in the concentration camps). A tomb was built here in 1950 to commemorate the victims of Nazism. It did not fare any better under the Communist regime when more gravestones were removed during the 1960s - 1970s[14]. The perimeter walls were broken down and the place was filled with waste and debris. In 1975, with the approval of the Municipal Council, the ceremonial hall was demolished; the house of the gravedigger was preserved since sheep were grazed on the site. After 1990, the cemetery was gradually repaired. Now only 350 monuments survive that have been identified and put back into their original position. Today, the cemetery is surrounded by industry with lorries parked next to the western wall and, in its entirety, the židovský hřbitov seems completely out of place with its surroundings.

---

[12] Jewish cemetery in České Budějovice. Wikipedia. https://cs.wikipedia.org/wiki/%C5%BDidovsk%C3%BD_h%C5%99bitov_v_%C4%8Cesk%C3%BDch_Bud%C4%9Bjovic%C3%ADch
[13] https://dbs.bh.org.il/place/ceske-budejovice
[14] Jewish Families from České Budějovice (Budweis), Bohemia, Czech Republic https://www.geni.com/projects/Jewish-Families-from-%25C4%258Cesk%25C3%25A9-Bud%25C4%259Bjovice-Budweis-Bohemia-Czech-Republic/15126

A Harvest of Sorrows: *Reflections on Disrespect*

[Stráž nad Nežárkou, 10 April 2011][15]

Walls and trees meld in lines,
vertical,
casting shadows
one on another,
moving slowly across,
marking days and time.
Sundials.

Bending,
touching;
corners reach around us,
inviting forward.
Of these
we know
the daily silence
overshadows not
the past
and what has happened here.
It is still happening.

Silver dollar,
Lunaria rediviva,
in stone
and life
gently shakes
upon April breeze.

---

[15] Note: Originally published on our blog:
http://czechfoodiesmn.blogspot.com/2011/04/jewish-cemetery-zidovsky-hrbitov-straz.html

Listen carefully
as stones speak,
rattle of horrors
past,
present.
Do walls
and locked gates
keep us from feeling?

Vinca minor
slithers silently
under gate,
catching our feet
wrapping the pulse of life:
of lives giving,
growing
yet kept apart.
Who can harvest
such sorrows?

Paths crossing
through forest
edge us in closer:
kept
at trunks' length.
Apart,
divided.

Glimpsing within
we see,
soak in
the chill of moist soil:
lean our stones
towards trees
that shade
and hold us up.

Until,
as trees,

as stones,
we blend as one.

In starkness
comes the night.

Figure 5. The eerie, barbed wire fencing atop the cemetery walls bar intruders from the family's garden (who live in the Hrobnický house) on the cemetery gravesites. Photo Credit: Mark Gilquist.

Background on the Stráž nad Nežárkou židovský hřbitov

Stráž nad Nežárkou, which mean "Guards Over the Nežárkou River", is located halfway between Jindřichův Hradec and Třeboň in southern Bohemia. The Rosenbergs built the castle there in the 13th century. It was later destroyed by lightning and rebuilt by the Lords of Stemberg. Jewish families settling here (1763-1837) included Freund, Schueller, Metzel, Loewy, Peisek, and Dubsky[16].

The židovský hřbitov started between 1810 and 1848 and served its purpose until WWII. The last burial took place in 1940 for Sophia Picková[16]. Currently, ~169 tombstones remain and many new ones have been added to replace the ones that were destroyed. Some epitaphs show great epigraphic culture of the local Jewish community. The Hrobnický house, a morgue, was restored in the early 21st century.

It is an easy židovský hřbitov to miss as we had driven past it multiple times and never seen it until one day, while Mark and I were exploring the town of Stráž nad Nežárkou, we looked across the fields from the old town and thought we saw a ceremonial hall! What's most disconcerting about this site is that a family now lives in the Hrobnický house, gardening in the back on the graves. They own the key to enter into the gates. It still jars my senses thinking about the modern-day desecration that is still occurring here: "it is still happening".

---

[16]https://cs.wikipedia.org/wiki/%C5%BDidovsk%C3%BD_h%C5%99bitov_ve_Str%C3%A1%C5%BEi_nad_Ne%C5%BE%C3%A1rkou

Overlooking

[Jindřichův Hradec, 24 Feb. 2011][17]

As we park
our Škoda,
a blind man and his dog
bark out
greetings.
We freeze inside.
Will they see us?
Aged redhead turns;
whitened canine nostrils' sensing.
As they pass,
we emerge.
Hellos exchange:
Dobrý den,
dobre pes.
We see
and
are seen.

Lynn, heavy with tripod,
vanishes over hill,
sliding towards Nežárka River,
past terraced gravestones,
climbing to overlook us
at curbside.

Mark and I depart from wheelchair,
meander along
where wall
drops in height at hillcrest.

---

[17] Note: Originally published on our blog,
http://czechfoodiesmn.blogspot.com/2011/03/visit-to-jewish-cemetery-zidovsky.html

Ivy entombs stately birches
with gentleness that ascends the wall
and holds us fast
to carpet the woods
in eternal green.
We lean as frost-heaved tombstones
against the wall,
letting chartreuse lichens
on our northern sides
grow.

Up here,
on Pejčoch Hill,
greyed concrete
of jarring Soviet lines
form windowed flats—
balcony vistas lined with red—
gone old of Bohemian coal soot years—
in each,
the windowed view
curtains elderly,
tucked sheer and thin,
we are closely watched.

We are seen.
And yet,
cemetery, walls
are not—in view.
Overlooked.

Over again,
repeatedly in walking us 'round,
he who in blindness with dog—
sees,
relooks,
we are here.

"How", you ask,
"do eyes that see

overlook
these walls?"

We the River Nežárka
on our way
in silence,
disappear.

Figure 6. Despite its stark contrast with aging Soviet flats, the cemetery corner wall –
while bedecked with English Ivy – has a road sign painted on it to warn passing autos of
the danger. Photo Credit: Neil Anderson.

Figure 7. Mark's feet repose at the base of the wall in the fallen leaves of yore. Photo Credit: Mark Gilquist.

Background on the Jindřichův Hradec židovský hřbitov

This city, literally at the center of Europe, was founded in ~1255 and became the economic hub of the continent during the 15th and 16th centuries[18] . The first Jews settled here in 1294. Many famous Jews were born here, e.g. conductor Kurt Adler (1907-1977 USA), opera singer-bassist National Theatre Karel Berman (1919-1995 Prague, Czech Republic) and painter Robert Piesen (1921-1977 Ein Hod, Israel).

The židovský hřbitov, a National Historic Landmark, may be one of the oldest Jewish cemeteries in the Czech Republic, founded in ~1400[18]. The site was once part of the manorial garden used as a training ground for falconry due to its hillside command over the river Nezarkou. In 1773, the cemetery was surrounded by a stonewall and also has a graveyard house and a modern ceremonial hall. The cemetery now has about 200 remaining tombstones; the oldest remaining one dates from 1638.

[18] židovský hřbitov https://www.hrady.cz/?OID=13785

Vying to Find the Gates Unlocked

[Česke Krumlov, 27 Feb. 2011][19]

In the winter burial of snows,
extant Czechs, tourists
flow 'round remnant lives
enfolded
on Cemetery Street.
Here,
salt traders,
smoked meat purveyors
stopped
on their way
to Linz, Austria,
bask in blush of pink,
cold winter's haze surround
summer castle tower
of Rosenbergs',
then Schwartzenbergs'.

While close by
hillside summer cottages,
garden thoughts
beneath Klet Mountain.
This Medieval town,
Vltava river,
old city walls
meander through lives
of summer's boaters,
        bustling, river-bent,
of dampness' chill on pussy willows
        springward unfolded,
of resplendent leaves
        bicolored maples, oaks,

---

[19] Note: Parts of this poem were originally published on our blog:
http://czechfoodiesmn.blogspot.com/2011/03/visit-to-jewish-cemetery-zidovsky_5752.html

        bookmarking fall upon our cheeks,
of silent swathing of snows
        on winter's edge:
voices of summer boaters,
Schwartzenbergs,
tourists,
Gentiles,
Jews
now fitfully buried.

We dance
uphill
to St. Vitis' church,
struggle eyes
upon the walls,
vying to find
the gates
unlocked.

Our hearts
are sinewed shut.

Figure 8. The snowed exterior to the cemetery walls we could not enter. Photo Credit: Mark Gilquist.

Background on the Česke Krumlov židovský hřbitov

The židovský hřbitov is located in the eastern part of Česke Krumlov close to the town cemetery on Cemetery Street. Ignaz Spiro, founder of the větřínských paper mills[20], established it in 1891. Funerals were held here until 1938.

After WWII, the cemetery fell into disrepair; the cemetery building stored hay and even horses were grazed therein. Overall, there are graves of people who came not only from Česky Krumlov, but also from at least 15 other villages and towns in nearby southern Bohemia[20].

[20] History of the Paper Mill in Větřní. Český Krumlov Tourism. Encyclopedia. http://www.encyklopedie.ckrumlov.cz/docs/en/region_histor_vetrni.xml

[Type here]

A Permanence of Remembering

[Hluboka nad Vltavou, 27 Feb. 2011]²¹

Not a word

from the Czechs,

whose heads bob along

above cemetery walls,

circling

Municky fish pond:

where naked oak branches

scrubbed clean

the ice

of snows.

In silence,

too,

those who in these gates lie.

Josef Metzel,

1880,

speaks for the others:

defaced,

ground down

by Nazi furor,

Soviet indifference.

---

[21] Note: Originally published on our blog,
http://czechfoodiesmn.blogspot.com/2011/03/visit-to-jewish-cemetery-zidovsky_05.html

Sharp edges
our senses jar.

Chartreuse green,
mossed living forms
line oaks
within the walls
of ivy.
One *Hedera helix*
climbing tenaciously
upwards,
oak bark enclenched,
holdfasts
above the wall.
Overlooking now
Benzina petrol station:
red-lined above
constant hum and bustle
of incoming cars,
petrol-hungry trucks.
Roaring us past.

Greyed,
sadly quiet
these walls,
threads of green proffered.
A richness arises

as we

place a small stone,

whitened of Hluboka's hunting castle walls:

carefully,

balancing time.

A permanence of remembering

from living.

Figure 9. Neil and Mark place a stone of quiet remembrance on top of a grave.
Photo Credit: Neil Anderson.

Figure 10. Inside the cemetery walls, a small blackbird rustles in the oak leaves at the base of the mossed trees and sings its heart out to us. Photo Credit: Mark Gilquist.

Background on the Hluboka nad Vltavou židovský hřbitov.

The židovský hřbitov in Hluboka was founded in ~1750. It is surrounded by a wall with ~190 tombstones (dated 1750 – 1941) mostly of Baroque and Classicist style.

Oddly enough in May 1945, in a twist of historic fate against the wall of this Jewish cemetery, 35 members of the former SS German army were executed by the Red Army. They were buried next to the cemetery, although the bodies were exhumed in 1994.

In Coming Here

[Třeboň, 10-11 Oct. 2010]

Softly turn car tires

as we descend from pavement

to gravel tracks:

edginess colored,

muted with newly fallen yellow

of

maple,

basswood.

Leaves embed our stop at forest edge

between

now,

then.

Here strong, tall brick run walls around the dead.

Could we,

in living,

breathe

what happened here?

A silent biker passes down the road,

'round the cornerstone,

we view

a once table, cart

bent now

beneath the weight of leaves.

Rusted hasp and lock of gate

stop us:

fall of headstones,

hammered, pulverized erasure

of those

here

then and now.

How can it be that we,

in love outstretched

bend of falling leaves?

Gently green the moss

fill cracks of mortar, hatred, brick, unrest.

Lay our hearts within the gates

so we,

beneath the leaves,

may keep the here, now

a part of them.

Figure 11. Green mosses, *Tetraphis pellucida*, adorn the destroyed bricks on top of the wall. Photo Credit: Neil Anderson.

Background on the Třeboň židovský hřbitov

The old Jewish synagogue still stands – just outside the walls of the old city of Třeboň. It was used for services until WWII, when it was remodeled as living quarters[22]. A family still lives in it today. Miraculously, three torahs that belonged to this Třeboň synagogue survived the war. They were recovered in Prague where the Nazi authorities had assembled torahs from all over the Czech lands. In 1964, the Jewish community of Westminster in Great Britain acquired 1,564 torahs from the Communist authorities[23]. Among these torahs were three from Třeboň which were later loaned to the United Kingdom (Pinner and Northwood Synagogue in the London metroplex) and the United States (New Bern, North Carolina; St. Louis, Missouri) synagogues – where they remain today.

---

[22] Trebon: Jindrichuv Hradec, Bohemia. International Jewish Cemetery Project. https://iajgscemetery.org/eastern-europe/czech-republic/trebon
[23] Jewish families from Třeboň (Wittingau), Bohemia, Czech Republic. Geni.com. https://www.geni.com/projects/Jewish-families-from-T%25C5%2599ebo%25C5%2588-Wittingau-Bohemia-Czech-Republic/15179

[Type here]

This nearly-forgotten židovský hřbitov (not the original one once located within the city walls) was founded in 1897-1900 and located east of the city in the woods. The last funeral occurred here in 1936. It is located on the cadastral area of the old village Clay. Its relative remoteness from Třeboň is due to the fact that it was permitted only outside the city and was out of the sight of the Christian population.

The ceremonial house dates from the founding of the cemetery and above the entrance stands the still legible inscription:

"Before death all are equal,

dear and venerated even those who are dear and venerated not."

The only one other Czech židovský hřbitov with brick walls like this one is in Brno. The decline of the Třeboň Jewish community is witnessed by the fact that, in 1910, there were 63 Jews here, while in 1921 there were just 29 Jews, mainly of Czech nationality. Tombstones occupy about half the area of the cemetery; the south side is empty. They are divided into four groups and the space is divided by a linden alley in the middle to the most significant site, the tomb of Louis Metzl, a textile trader from Třeboň and chairman of the local Jewish community. His three sons and most of their families were tortured in concentration camps.

Finale, May 2011, Třeboň

The židovský hřbitov are in various states of restoration or neglect but the remnant destruction by the Nazis or current-day vandals are inescapable, filling us with wonder, horror, grief, and amazement of what survived…be it plants, stone walls, gravestones, Ceremonial Houses and the like.

We trust that you will be inspired reading the poems and viewing the eternality of spirit, repairing & rebuilding while pausing in your tracks at human ingratitude for diversity and difference.

Back Cover. Neil Anderson (left), Mark Gilquist (center) and Lynn Silverman (right) join hands outside the Třeboň židovský hřbitov in celebration of our year-long Fulbright venture to experience and record, through our photography and my poetry, our journey to visit as many židovský hřbitov throughout Bohemia and Moravia as possible. We assembled a fresh flower/foliage floral design and hung it on the gate near the Rosenberg rose; a subsequent photograph recorded this as the cover for this book. Photo Credit: Mark Gilquist.

www.ingramcontent.com/pod-product-compliance
Lightning Source LLC
Chambersburg PA
CBHW042124080426
42733CB00002B/12